Rites of Strangers

The Virginia Commonwealth University Series
for Contemporary Poetry

Walton Beacham, General Editor

Moving Out,
by David Walker, 1976
The Ventriloquist,
by Robert Huff, 1977

Rites of Strangers

Phyllis Janowitz

University Press of Virginia
Charlottesville

THE UNIVERSITY PRESS OF VIRGINIA
Copyright © 1978 by the Rector and Visitors
of the University of Virginia

First published 1978

Library of Congress Cataloging in Publication Data

Janowitz, Phyllis.
  Rites of strangers.

  (The Virginia Commonwealth University series for contemporary poetry)
  I. Title. II. Series: Virginia Commonwealth University. The Virginia Commonwealth University series for contemporary poetry.
PS3560.A534R5 811'.5'4 78–16729 ISBN 0–8139–0797–7

Printed in the United States of America

For my mother

Contents

Acknowledgments

The author and publisher wish to thank the following magazines for permission to reprint certain poems:

The *Andover Review* for "Falling into the Moment" and "Their Town"

The *Atlantic Monthly* for "The Wait"

The *Blacksmith Anthology* for "Wilbur"

Centering for "Dancing with Mr. D.," "Moving in America," and "Veal"

Connections for "Celeste Counting Down"

Esquire for "Madeleine" and "Soon the Final Decree"

Event for "Veal." Published in *Event*, vol. 2, no. 2.

Fireweed for "Mr. Hinman's Wife"

The *Hartford Courant* for "#13" from "Revolutionary Lulu"

Harvard Magazine for "Elegy for Mrs. Lucky"

The *Hawaii Review* for "A Man and a Woman"

The *Nation* for "Monterey"

Oyez Review for eight poems from "Revolutionary Lulu": "#1," "#2," "Lulu's Dream," "#4," "Heathrow Airport," "Letters," "Everyone Gives Lulu Advice," and "Lulu Wonders if She Will Ever"

The *Paris Review* for "Luncheon at the Marshalls"

Ploughshares for "Veal"

Poetry Northwest for "At the Center for Displaced Persons"

Prairie Schooner for "Coming of Age"

The *Radcliffe Quarterly* for "Reunion with Jake at Still Pond Creek." Copyright © 1978 by Radcliffe College. Reprinted with permission of the *Radcliffe Quarterly*.

Red Cedar Review for "A Cool Day in the Sun"

The River Styx for "Lang Anh Says Goodbye to Her Daughter"

Shenandoah for "Facing It." Copyright 1978 by Washington and Lee University, reprinted from *Shenandoah*: The Washington and Lee University Review, with the permission of the Editor.

Twelfth Key for five poems from "Mia's Masquerade": "The Way She Lived in Pompeii," "She Rides a Ferris Wheel Every Night," "Retrospective," "Intermission," and "She's Becoming a Singular Person"

Willow Springs for "Change of Address" (originally "Moving in America")

Wind/Literary Journal for "The Hermit"

I wish to express my gratitude to the Radcliffe Institute, the MacDowell Colony, and the National Endowment of the Arts, whose support enabled me to write these poems, and to the many friends who inspired me.

In the imagination we are from henceforth (so long as you read) locked in . . . the classic caress of author and reader. We are one. Whenever I say "I" I mean also "you."

—*William Carlos Williams*

One

Luncheon at the Marshalls

We are ten minutes late. They
are very sweet, hiding their
rage under pink sugar, boiled

icing that pains the teeth.
We admire the latest blackened
addition to the ancestral

collection, a mustachioed toad
encased in a shroud of grease.
The Aubussons are covered with dust.

*Sweet satin, how I would like
to lie in all that money.
I'd know what to do with it.*

They've had a pay toilet
for their guests installed.
It only costs a quarter.

Now the car with the chauffeur
has driven off without mother.
Again! The drawing room is

steeped in a drift of baby
dandruff. At least the baby has
stopped his lisps and gurgles.

They've resolved to have no
more of his kind in the house.
They'll put up a sign saying

"Rich People Live Here"
and ask their guests to bring
their own refreshments or go

hungry. At the picnic table
we open our box of Kentucky
Fried Chicken. A cloud

resembling a eunuch watching
a harem watches us eat.
The sky darkens. The hounds

hang around whining, begging.
Their ribs are showing.
A cold drizzle sifts down.

Reunion with Jake at Still Pond Creek

We are becoming martyrs to our spirits,
you and I. Every time I see you,
you are thinner, listless, eating less.
You have given up breakfast and dinner,
sometimes indulging in a lettuce leaf
at noon. I know you aim to disappear.
What we both want is sensation without
shame or fear. And now I am bored
by sex, washing my hair, my clothes,
the bathroom scarred with drying underwear.
The time a body takes. The waste. Forests
of Kleenex. Six ibis for an acre of grain.
The pull of gravity shrinking us, drying
out the tissues of the brain. Bodiless
we could go anywhere. For how could we
transgress? To fly with no fear of falling,
no planes, schedules; no one inspecting our
baggage, dirty socks spilling from plastic
sacks, condoms, Tampax, the ungraceful
reminders our bodies insist on. I'm afraid
this flesh will always be too solid for us,
Jake. Your cigarettes reveal that. I take
up smoking when we are together. We eye
each other through the clouds we make.

A Cool Day in the Sun

You gently dust the skin
    from the blowfish
like a cobweb. It is left
    headless, small and white
with silver fins.

There is no end to the patterns
    that can be made on water.
Ours is an iron fretwork
    we impose upon the waves;
when we leave it will
    still be there,

like the water and sky
    or the cool bar of the flute
you play, leaving
    a permanent stain on the sand,

or the bird
    sitting on a rock
since yesterday.

I feel tied to the blanket
    on the beach,
waiting for a different bird
    or until you get hungry
and we go inside.

If I were here alone
    I would stay forever
until my skin
    slipped off like feathers
and my bones
    bleached, and I disappeared
into the sand

or blew over the water.
So effortless, painless,
    natural.

Monterey

The children rise, round loaves,
fat and brown. They rise
until there is no room in the house
anymore, until they
spill over, and there is no one home
to add on rooms
or push the walls out for them.

At the coast, by the rough edge of the ocean,
trees change shape with the wind's
direction; they don't die.
There are certain distortions, flat tops,
and the branches are bent back,
away from the water.

The children arrange pebbles and shells
in circles under the trees.
They play games beneath the crooked branches.
They think this is the way
trees should look, like puzzles
reaching out,
and no one has to solve them.

Moving in America

There isn't enough money
to pay the rent, or too much
money for too little house.
This happens once a year.
It is announced in the papers.
Everyone packs garden shears,
carpet sweepers, dog collars
and old eye glasses.
One time the moving van
comes to move us at 6 A.M.
One time the movers
arrive with our furniture
at midnight. I could tell you
stories. They have done
research that proves that 4
years of an average American's
life are spent moving from one
establishment to the next.
You bring the phonograph
to a store in your new
neighborhood. When you go
to pick it up, it is in
a hundred pieces. No one
knows how to put it together.
There is no charge.
Your coat comes back from
the cleaners, full of strange
holes. There is no charge.
Neighborhood children trample
on your rose bushes.
You're afraid to complain.
The territory is unfamiliar.
It will never be yours.

Coming of Age

From the windows of our new
home we catch glimpses of them.
At first only a skitter
in the back yard, a squirrely
shadow, but not furry.
A hairless tail. We notice
the holes becoming numerous
around the rabbit cages.

Three of us, two children and me.
The children, one of each sex,
battle over mangled dolls, trains
without wheels. When the nuclear
family divides, the survivors
tire easily. We are more
tightly bonded to each other.

They grow bolder. We recognize
an entire tribe coming
up from the holes, pushers,
taking over. A number of babies.
One runs across my foot.
Another lugs a heavy dog
bone through the grass.
They are whiskered, frisky,
familiar. I find them not
unattractive but am afraid
to go into the yard. The Board
of Health man has a deep, froggy
voice. Reassuring. If there
were any other way, I would never
do this. My insomnia is worse.

The children have frequent
nightmares, crying out in their
sleep, high-pitched wails, weeks
after the ritual murder. Although
the way the poison works, we don't
see any corpses. The back yard
is deserted. We fill in the holes.

A Man and a Woman

At five miles an hour thick
huge snowflakes drift up
in the light from the high-
beam, opposing gravity
and all obtuse rules.

I think of the two of us,
mirrors who admire, glitter,
reflect. Never touch.
Something is missing.
You discover other women

are novelties, their curves
stretch you or make you
look broader, muscular.
You say they are more
exciting than me. I couldn't

agree with you more. Now,
learning that one deep inhalation
can make me forget you,
I giggle like wind chimes.
Other men are charming, snow-

covered branches waving at me.
I drive home alone, white
as a bride, watching
snow flowers
float through the windshield
into my eyes.

Revolutionary Lulu

1. When Trouble Comes

When trouble comes to Lulu's dad
and mum it comes between them,
sawing the air, loving a battle.

TeeVee rattles in its box, magazines,
papers, tiresome weights; plastic shapes
in darkness reveal screws, wheels.

. . . a breakdown of communications here.
That's it! That's it! begins the breaking
up. The medium is them, their lips are sealed.

2. Lulu's Mum

Lulu's mum: About your father, you see
there's a relationship he has with the house,
the car, that he's never had with me.
The way he fondles materials, rubs
the grains of wood and metal, explores
interiors, puts his hand into glove
compartments, dresser drawers.
For nineteen years I wanted to lock
those things up, hold his socks rolled
in balls on my lap, pretend to be
a suitcase or cabinet so he'd touch me
like that, his hands caring and deft,
the ends of his fingers electric.

3. Lulu's Dream

Driving along as usual thinking
about sun, moon and her private radio
blasting stars from the dashboard,
she almost runs over a man, a woman,
on the road, comes to a jolting
halt, brakes singing underfoot.
Who is it? Why Dad, why
Mum. She drives on, watching
through the rear-view mirror.
Oh no! Like London Bridge, Dad's
fallen down. And worse. Mum's
tumbled too. She's sprawled,
a pitiful bundle of rags on asphalt,
waving her hand for attention.
Lulu knows neither one of them
can get up alone. She turns
the car around.

4. Bip. Bip. Bip.

Bip.Bip.Bip.Bip.Bip.Bip.Bip.
Lulu thinks she's typing fast.
Alas she fails the typing test.
No job for Lulu this summer.
Her father divorces her.

Jobless, worthless, Lulu
whines a lot, further devaluating
her currency. Her face breaks
out. Now all is lost.
She is not even American.
She will go to England
to seek her fortune. Like Dick
Whittington she may become
thrice Lord Mayor of London.

Lulu has been told anything
is possible. She believes
she will marry a Rolling Stone
and never gather moss again.

Lulu's father sternly
returns her water bed
from the house he shares
with his girlfriend. Forgetting
the heater. The water bed,
unwatered, dries up
like a raisin in the sun.

5.   Heathrow Airport

Deplaning, she feels
the shock of a body arriving
long after a brain. A jolt
of oxygen which is not just
jet-lag hums through her veins,
makes her feet quite light.
She bounces along a cobbled street.

From a niche in a building
a frowsy-haired archetypal
waif appears, offers
to carry her bags. His white
face whiter than this page,
he resembles a gullible
troll, or an ugly Oliver

Twist. At this great
find, Lulu's heart leaps
up like a fish. O Dickens!
O 19th Century! Can people
be homesick their whole lives
for places they've never been?
Lulu now knows that they can.

6. Letters

Lulu's father writes,
"Dear Daughter . . ." His girl-
friend has left him.
She has moved to an apartment,
taking her baby, yowling

Aviva, with her. Lulu
is jubilant. At last
she is no longer a semi-
orphan. She writes
long letters from
London. "I am becoming

mature. I have two
boyfriends. One owns
a Triumph (green),
the other an Alfa Romeo."
Triumph is better
in some ways, but

Alfa Romeo takes her
to interesting parties
where she eats avocado,
mackerel, pâté, and
other British delicacies.
Lulu's father feels

she is finally finding
herself. She writes,
"It's true I care
too much for money,
clothes, elegant
possessions. I have made

up my mind to change.
I will be less
materialistic, I know,
as soon as I get
everything I want."

7.   No Things but in Ideas

Only once was Lulu in that
garden shaped like a maze where tall

gardeners wear top hats and tip
them, saying, "This is that. That is

that." Never wearying a bit,
or wearing out their welcomings,

they clip undiminished hedges—
a rusty sun disk sticks at noon.

What is Lulu looking for? Does

hibiscus forget? Or twisted
green ivy? Heat makes hundreds

of crabs march from the sea into
a nearby, empty hotel, to rest

in shadow until summer's end.
All summer Lulu reads, riding

low, neck curved, head down, the way
a loon circling a lake scans for fish.

8.   Encounter

Lulu believes the mailman
has been muted by the C.I.A.
so he will not reveal any

secrets. He arrives with
a stack of letters and cards
from Guatemala, Tierra del

Fuego, Newark. Shepherds
regard the Mediterranean
as if it had just bloomed

ice-blue in the desert.
A tiger lily lifts a jeweled
finger. The mailman still

stands at the door. His eyes
are twin stoves Lulu won't
look into, she has a fear

of burning. She says,
"I don't know what to do
when you stare at me so."

She leans over and whispers
into his ear, "For all I
know, you're imagining how

I'd look without my clothes."
If he could speak, Lulu would
choose him above all, because

he is creator and mender of
wounds, and because he has wings
on his heels. If he could speak,

Lulu is sure it would be in
plainsong, then he would dance
her all over the room, before

folding her fluttering words into
silence, like an eloquent letter
on blank sheets of paper, like

a day lily closed for the night.

9.   The Arrangement

She dreams a photographer
comes to shoot her picture,
Lulu in her wedding dress,
holding all those dead daisies
and afraid to move. She sees
he has no arms.
She is
speechless.

At a restaurant table
her mother says,
"I don't want you
thinking.
I want you to
relax, be joyous."

Lulu butters a roll,
but the strings
are cut. Her ideas
float over her head
in enormous balloons,
causing the waiter
to pour icewater
onto the tablecloth.

Lulu knows
if she goes on
like this
she will not
have any friends.

People say things—
"Whatsa matter,
cat got your tongue?"
Lulu only giggles,
but her answer
rises in black and white
for the world to read.

10. Everyone Gives Lulu Advice

Her eyes are empty teacups, waiting
for a flow of words. She is
a challenge to the wise. Messengers
go to all borders of the brain's
left side for aphorisms to be
poured into Lulu's hopeful
head. Surely someone can help
her crack the code of life,
a mystery maze of clipped shrubs
separating her from the world.

Flora's father, Mr. Fyrmapple,
who knows all about kings
and queens, has a dream; a person
in long white robes is writing
in a book of gold. Mr. Fyrmapple
asks, "What are you writing in that
book of gold?" And the person
replies, "The names of those
who look after Lulu."

The next day Mr. Fyrmapple
approaches Lulu in the library.
His round face appears ready
to explode and scatter pieces
of red skin about the room.
He suggests, "Lulu, you'd best
get married before you're 21.
A girl like you with an unknown
background. A man would only
want you when you're young.
You're lonesome, Lulu. You need
security. But once you go
too far with a man—just once—
everything is lost. No one
will ever respect you again."

This fear Lulu is feeling—
her heart a heavy jogger
in her chest—perhaps this,
at last, is love. Her eyes
buzz over Mr. Fyrmapple's face
as if he's a fragrant gardenia.

11.   Lulu Wonders if She Will Ever

Become a mellow lady,
trailing feathers and fish
scales and singing
in the afternoons. Her friend,
the silver Bentley
she had hoped to bring back
to the States, confesses
he's worried about his suspension,
he's considering becoming a woman,
and his mother needs him at home.
Hands of unknown origin

squeezing her waist,
pains in her legs from growing.
Rover the goat, who died
small and sweet, after
chewing her hair as she slept.
Lulu should have been spared
these griefs. Lulu
should have sprung from Cardin's
at twenty, molded in bisque,
draped in chiffon, her eyes
glazed with perfection,
her eyelids on gold hinges
swinging open and shut
at intervals marked by the sun.

12.   The Fire-Eater

It is the eye at the slats, the sprinkler
between her and the door, the doorbell

that doesn't ring. Who is the mat
welcoming? The dog draws back pale

lips, his teeth are clotted with tartar.
It is that no one is ever home but her.

It is the meeting that never takes place,
although she is prepared, although

she has Xeroxed the notes and someone
has blown dry her falling hair.

The excuses line up like three-legged
cats she feeds and forgives.

Her invitation to the Christmas Ball
must have been lost in the mail.

"Oh yes," she agrees. "That must be it."
The butcher overcharges her. He knows

what she's afraid of. When her eggs
are yolkless, she's sure it's not

accidental. She tries to complain,
but her words won't connect, her sentences

refuse to hang together. Army ants
are eating her brain as she sleeps.

She should expect nothing. She should be
bovine. For two sticks she'd give you

what she never outgrows. It is hope
keeps her burning like an old wood stove.

13.   Laughter Sets Her Going

Laughter sets her going like a roll
of drums. Even at her own wedding,
consumed by an unspeakable desire

to guffaw. Wuff, wuff, it would have
erupted, sudden dog, her ears pointy,
fur on her face, and the blue-suited

young man, so serious at her side,
would he have gone home armored by his
mother and father, the calliope playing

"Oh, how we danced on the night we
were wed," and everyone long vanished,
with her forever outcast from such

circles. Oh, if it had happened!
What then? Would the laughter have
come again, this time in the form

of a crow, issuing its caw from her
astonished mouth as the defeated trio
stepped down, her shoulders shaking,

her neck pulled in. Would she have
uttered her unseemly croaks and then
flown after them, a tarbrush of feathers,

the gold ring in her beak?

TWO

Their Town

At the meeting everyone waits
for the stranger to speak
of cool arms, thighs, silk

flesh in motion. He sips
a bourbon and water, dries
his lips with a tiny paper

napkin, and says, "The average
American moves twelve times
in a lifetime." Disappointing.

They have always lived in this
damp climate, in this town,
everything's gray with mold,

shoes, power tools, children.
People are used to it. They
are quick to fill the holes

between words, when they feel
their veins turn gray. Only a
stranger might wonder how they

can cut corn and sweet clover
or watch a football float over
a goalpost and never mention

the difficult breathing, dreams
they have in daylight, how
every weekday in season the air

is clouded with falling birds.

The Wait

No use trying to hurry it. It

will arrive when it's ready. Nine months

you say? Then you cannot delay it.
It has already decided what

you will name it. It will push you off
your chair, take your place at the table.

It is planning to sleep in your bed,
wear your pajamas. In due time it

will feed you rat poison, or run an
exhaust pipe into your room. Oh do

not weep. All is planned and natural.

Even now it is curled in a fist.

Thumb in mouth it is laughing at you.

A Family Portrait

This is a house the wind blows through

And this is a child
who doesn't speak
as he rocks in a chair
with a wicker seat
but who grunts or shrieks
and can't be reached
who will need years
of costly care
who never leaves
a three-story house
the house the wind blows through

And this is the red
eye of the mother
blurred with love
and rage as she
watches the child
who never speaks
but rocks back
and forth like
a pendulum
or bangs his head
in a rhythmic beat

Here is the father
with bitter mouth
who loves the mother
with reddened eyes
and fears the child
who costs so much
in the house the wind
blows through

This is the drafty heart of the house:
an unspeakable room
the child in a chair
rocking and rocking

away from the man
with blood in his eyes
the woman with bitter-
sweet mouth
not knowing
how far their child
will rock or why

as they love and rage
faster and harder
each day they find less
to say to each other

in the house the wind blows through

Madeleine

The last time he saw her she was eight,
strawberry curls spilled down her back.
Those days he'd pull squares of divinity

out of her ears to make her giggle.
He still has a moustache and a worried look,
sometimes éclairs burn, sweet rolls fail

to rise, angel food falls. Often
the sales girls, slow and sticky, give
the wrong change. There are problems,

he tells her, handing her a cookie, even
though she is covered with icing and under
her flawless white shell the cake, rich

and dark, is well hidden. He knows
who she is, for years in his dreams he has
molded her into his finest meringue,

his most excellent *mousse aux marrons*,
although in other dreams she is
nothing but an ordinary tart, someday

his pastry tube will put on
the finishing touches, pink sugared
roses, rivulets of whipped cream.

Veal

I love to watch the butcher
wipe the sharp
blade on his
apron stained
with fresh blood. I'm
going to marry him

WHAM

the side of beef split open
he tenderly spreads
it like a woman's legs
between smeared fingers
stroking the cold smoothness

from his fingertips
          bloody red
drops on the floor spotting the sawdust there
fluffs of fat lie covered decently
the meat is red and lean

He is huge with the scissors and knives of love
and I so refined so shrinking violet
am in love in love
and bite the inside of my mouth
to taste the hot spurts
of blood

swallowing
the sudden salt

WHAM

            the chopper
right through   the bone
the knife   cleaving clean

        any thickness desired

as beautiful as birth
as normal
as bloody

Again he wipes the knife
on his apron
thin thin slices scooped
with swollen hands onto pieces of
white paper
weighs them

no fat   no fat

arms thick as a roast
he lets my mother
keep the bills
for a year
like love letters
on a spike in the kitchen

Dancing with Mr. D.

I was a tender bud tango-
ing with a moustache in a glen plaid
jacket, back and forth, until
I was palsied as a peony
and my petals were popping all over
the floor. Between dances he passed
out brochures from Eternal Acres.
For a small fee: *Silvery*
Lawns, an Incinerator
and a Gold Plated Urn
in every back yard.

O put an end to lies and
self-deceits he sang in my ear, my angel,
as we zigged and zagged into
the potted palms. Life's absurd,
a game, yet laughter rocks down
the years like Grandma, who will crochet
bright squares, yellow and red,
for our babies; they will
speak in tongues that only
Grandma understands.

I could have gone on sliding
and gliding, but he left, saying I was
immature and did I have a gray-
haired sister? In the mirror
my face was a fresh apple no one wise
would bite into, and even though his smile
sliced across my wrists, nothing
was visible, and I knew
how to smile too. (And
I still do.)

O my peddler, dear seller
of plots and toadstools, I am waiting
for you to return, so we can
polka until my quivering parts
shake into shadows, the padding falls
from my hands. When my eyes sink down
in my head, when my skull forms
a lipless grin, you undoubtedly
will come to agree that
I am not too young, not
too young, not too young.

The Funeral Director's Wedding

Is planned to include every tradition,
A nubile bride, vintage champagne,
A cake in tiers, a simple reception.
Mr. Fortune has a new cravat,

An old tuxedo, a sprightly carnation,
A career riveting his attention,
Future wages commensurate.
He is immaculate.
Nothing is forgotten or forgiven.
Only a few have received invitations,

Those who call themselves "The Chosen."
And the bride? Shy slip
Who will yield her life to him,
Wearing the gauze of a reflection?
All eyes on him, his mien, perfection.
A familiar threnody begins.

Ta Ta Da Dum. Ta Ta Da Doo.
The carpeted aisle is not wide
But leads to an altar where ends reside
In beginnings. Mr. Fortune knows
That while some may come and some may go,
The procession must be dignified.

But now, "Let be be finale of seem,"
Mr. Fortune quotes to his bride,
Gently removing the veils that hide
The director of the final dream.

My Story

They have arrested Lionel three times
for wife-beating. Everyone knows
he loves me. Now free, he touches me.
A hairy hand holds a Gillette
to my throat, drags it across
in a silver arc. My head rolls off.
A team of green surgeons sews it
back on while a hundred years of pie-
faced strumpets trundle by.

I wake, smiling, strung with cobwebs.
"A miracle!" The medicine men, elated,
fling their frocks on the floor.
They dance a stately dance together.
Yet when I begin to order my body,
it will not obey, walks in a different
direction, attempts to paint a landscape
on an easel. Sunset. Rocks. I never
could draw. The hands

they say are mine ignore me, clawing
the canvas until they have painted
a marvelous twilight, mercurial clouds
leaking crescents of blood. I watch
the fingers, absurd and driven birds
refusing to be reasonable. How they
forget what is left of me (a smile,
a skull) skimming into evening as if
there are no connections.

Mr. Hinman's Wife

has been a nuisance for years,
always overcooking

the eggs. Now she resembles
a particle of yellow dust

no one can catch. She won't
answer the phone or visit

old friends. She has become
a bumblebee, one of the hive

humming a tune over the petunias.
Someday Mr. Hinman will hear

a tiny motor rumbling, feel
a twinge in his arm. A small

raised spot will itch fiercely.
It will keep him from forgetting

her, when he drinks his coffee,
when he reads the *Times*.

Soon the Final Decree

Her arrow-straight hair will not escape
from its bow. Her glasses will never
slide down her nose. From now on
her base will be Boston. She will tell
the passengers tied to their seats
how she and the captain are going to be
divorced. Her voice has made up its mind.

On Dumbo, a great gray beast, we head
north, over a fog where turtles
swim in mud which is neither sky
nor sea. The turtles are only four
inches long. Their small paws are webbed.
Their shells are surprisingly sensitive.
We know which way they are going.

Who can tell what an elephant will do?
In the hook of Dumbo's trunk, Captain
Wright swings like a broken bell,
as if he's drunk or piloting
an invisible bomber running out of fuel.
Soon his shoes will drop from his feet,
two birds plummet to earth. Oh blue
stewardess with red striped cuffs,
we hope you enjoy your flight.

Mia's Masquerade

1. The Way She Lived in Pompeii

She was sedate, tame as a heavily tranquilized
mental patient, folding laundry, children
into rubbers and coats, drugged by cooking odors,
paying no attention in the A & P
to the fury of housewives as she dreamily
walked off with their half-filled carts,
blandly exchanging groceries when pursued.

She dozed light as a toothpick on a foam rubber
mattress, listening for the first child's wail.
(Her sleeping husband chased naked nymphs
over dune and dale, kicking up
pink hooves, often his neighing woke her.)

For years meekly waiting, the heat rising
in her belly like the sun, making it
swell in a kind of false pregnancy,
and one day a gusher of black lava rushing out
through her mouth, her nose, covering them all.
The perfectly preserved bodies can be seen
in lucite boxes, the tourists chatter and stare.
The only survivor has begun her travels.

2. She Rides a Ferris Wheel Every Night

for months, the wheel pink and green
in a confectioner's carnival, sugared
leaves and roses sprinkling her hair
and the merry-go-round music blaring
like a hot summer day. On the ground

her moon-faced friend, the tap dancer,
sings, *I think I'm falling*
    in love with you.
Don't, she dreams, his love a burden,
a white dog in a wicker basket he wants
her to carry for him, an unbearable
weight to take on her circlings.

Then, nothing, nine nights in a row
she wakes empty handed, groping
with blind fingertips for what she has
lost: her unborn children, the color
of their hair, their sex, even
their names have vanished. The days
and nights are a summer without flowers,
a limbo land where dreams play hide-
and-go-seek like children not to be
found, the dog runs away and doesn't
return, and the question *is he dead*
is he dead dances with motes of sun
up the stairs step by step, comes
to the bed each morning and licks
her dangling hand.

3.   She Becomes Familiar With

a scenario written just for her
in which she is chief star
also the most interesting
character, with a great stash
of masks and a script that says
    You must be what you are.

Bit players come in, go out,
unreal as walking vegetables:
a parsnip, a Brussels sprout,

cabbages with legs and tongues.
Afterwards she can't remember
the pantomime performed.

Those unborn children are more
distinct, the ones she hoped
to show off, giggling and shy:
a line of wind-up toys, acrobats,
clowns, a whole circus to parade
in front of an astounded audience.

The calliope playing
    BOOMP BOOMP da da da da
    Bump Bump Bump Bump
    BOOMP BOOMP da da da da
    Bump Bump Bump Bump
    da da da DUM

Now the children wait
silent, stopped in the wings,
expecting a signal. They think
someone will pound on the floor.
Surely someone will whistle.
Knowing they'll never appear

at all, she rehearses her new role,
exercising, warming up,
until words, gestures, mood,
bubble through neon tubing
in loops of lurid purple light,
shouting her name at the crowd.

4.   Retrospective

Gradually her memory shadows
grow luminous around
the edges, messages
from the past glow
greenly in the dark.
Now she knows what happened
to the midget who complained
about cramped quarters and frequently,
bitterly, kicked her in the belly.
But where are the nights she slept
with her stomach turned to the ceiling
because he protested if she tried to sleep
on him? Those weeks were flutes and piccolos.
Those weeks were rock and roll. If she could
find them in some huge storage area, she would
mount them like pictures against a white
background, an exhibition to be murmured
over by elegant voyeurs of art,
or project them in a film
against a fading wall,
until the separate frames
became one vast stomach
mountain lifted
to the ceiling
as an eternal offering.

5.   Intermission

The two men make love with only
their eyes. The lobby is crowded.
They wear identical pin-striped suits.
In the middle of all the standing
bodies, they are close, almost touching.

Voices gradually thicken and rise
like smoke in the heavy air. The two

men say nothing. The woman watches
from outside their circle of chalk,
listening motionless as a rabbit
in tall grass. Her long hair, round
body, frighten them. She is dangerous.
She wants to say, Listen, here I am,
look at me, touch me with your cool hands,
let me swim underwater with you.

Her thoughts disturb them. They are
forced to handcuff her, remove her
to a small cell, shove her in, locking
the heavy door. She looks out through
the bars, invisible. If nobody sees her,
could she be dead? The guard, a woman
with stiletto eyes, wears a tight red
satin skirt, brings her water, a little
bread, stays to watch her eat.

6.   Every Evening Her Guilt

is brought out
and spread on the floor
between them, dirty
underpants the dog
has a mad desire for,
he'd chew holes
if he could in the crotch.

This is a trial
where the criminal
has been guilty
since birth, due to a poor

choice of chromosomes,
while the verdict of *guilty*
is a sensual thrill that topples
her city, leaving her land
a playground for mutations
of slashers and stranglers
with unusual hang-ups.

No more handholding.
Black-frocked, the judge raps
his gavel three times.
Life or one hundred years,
whichever comes first,
is to be spent in solitary.
The bells toll:
three black tears.

7.   Learning to Live with Less

Footsteps of dead friends tap like rain
over the ceiling of her cellar room.
She calls until her voice is gone.
Toadstools are sprouting, leaping about;
their flat tops, shriveled and edged
with brown, resemble her grandmother's
frayed lace collars. At night she hears,

> *Father we thank thee for the night,*
> *And for the blessed morning light,*

Grandma singing lullabies,
a thin, cracked croon.

She'd love to hack off pieces of herself.
One day two fingers at the joint,
another time, her smallest toe. If there
were less of her, there'd be less longing
for yellow marigolds or the indigo blue

of a flute quartet. Photographs float by,
an old one of her sister. She remembers
the two of them hiding a lame cat for hours
under the bed; only its meowing gave it away.

> *Thou shalt wake when God will,*
> *from thy slumber so still.*

Her mind, deprived of stimuli, feeds
on flutterings. A dark moth becomes
a vulture; the rush of its wings, a weight
added to the strained pumping of her heart.

8.   She's Becoming a Singular Person

On the wall a Xeroxed notice reads:

> *Welcome*
> *to the living theater.*
> *We've been acting here forever,*
> *and all of us*
> *bad actors,*
> *paranoid, possessed, sleeping*
> *in coffins,*
> *in cages, hiding from the ticking sun*
> *and the white foxes*
> *running on the beach.*

She glides back and forth,
following and pursued by her shadow,
through a mirror observing
her elderly double, or else
it's a baby, gone in the teeth.

She'd be a blur of feathers
heading south, if she could escape

her kind—a dancer dangling
over obstacles, who doesn't know
why every solo starts at rest
or ends with the body a tight
scroll, and motionless,

but understands that each atom
has a pattern of its own, and must
perform with others on the mirror's
tinseled surface, before her twin
selves meet or reflection begins.

Wilbur

The watch on his wrist and his pulse are ticking together,
softly. Only Wilbur can hear them whisper,
"Go home Willie. No one wants you here."

Willie's wispy as filigree, resilient as wire.
And he's always on time. As if they were made for each
    other,
the watch on his wrist and his pulse are sticking together.

Wilbur would like to assume a more casual air,
but his flimsy grin wears thin when he hears people swear,
"Go home Willie. No one wants you here."

He arranges to meet you under the clock at Zayre's.
And you're late. Or don't come. Maybe you don't even
    care.
The watch on his wrist and his pulse keep talking together.

Willie's no Weeper. He hopes that sooner or later
someone will touch him, someone too tender to sneer,
"Go home Willie. No one wants you here."

He can flit like a finch, a bunch of small bones and feathers,
but he knows how to wait. He'll wait for an hour or
    forever,
the watch on his wrist and his pulse beating together.

If blood leaks from his veins while he waits somewhere,
Willie will just go on waiting. He won't really care
that the watch on his wrist and his heart are unwinding
    together.
"Go home Willie no one wants you here."

The Hermit

Letters I might have written
    slide off the waxed
finish of pages, become
    low hedges. In my

room I watch walls
    wrinkle, huge tears
trickle from painted leaves.
    In dreams it is not

wings that keep me
    flying but gerbils and
chameleons, small
    creatures make me feel

important: a hunchback
    snail creeping to suck
leaves, and one night
    a mouse uses a broom

to sweep snow from
    the fence posts. I am
disturbed by a
    trifling loss. Where

is my yellow umbrella?
    A morning bottle of milk,
frozen, slips from my
    cold hand, becomes

a thousand crystal morsels.
    Consolation prize:
I dream of someone breathing
    like a spider in my ear.

Celeste Counting Down

1. Portents

Black flappings skirt her head. Her horoscope
warns *Take extra precautions*. She sticks
to what she knows. Potatoes slow baked.
Turnips and peas. Breeze over the floor
with a broom. Industry confounds the evil ones.
Cleanliness makes them uneasy. She sits down
to scan the obituaries, rises to put
a dirty load in the machine. The wind
lifts as she sighs, rain streams across the blinds.
In her washer high-pitched voices squeak and scream.

2. An Instinct like Love

This is the terrible dream of sparrows
a ceaseless fluttering to fill
the mouths of their young
Celeste   with five of her own
could write it in her sleep   aching
all-night flights and never enough
to shut the stretched beaks   as if carved
from wood   cuts between the feathers
invisible
leaving a trail of blood
the terrible dream of women   exhausted
moving through sleep   fearful as birds

3.   Celeste Dines with Cherie, an Aging Lady of the Night

Turn my thoughts from journey's end,
keep the pleasure on the road
                    from disappearing.
Take, oh take away your friend,
the silent one that you regard
                    as so endearing.

Why do you have a skull in your
dining room? I can't enjoy
a morsel here. Those holes where
black irises once gleamed glare
        at me over silverware,
across flowering cups, plates
and napkins, with more intensity
than any eyes. Before I'd keep
        a cranium as a pet I'd pat
some flesh around that bony head,
give him a nose, lips, the kind
that move. Cherie, next time
        you invite me for dinner let
your other guest come complete
with torso and a pair of arms
and legs. You could make him
look elegant in a gray pin-
striped suit. We could even
        pretend it was a party.

4.   Hospital

    The terminal. People silently consult
schedules, a penthouse of passengers who
take off without groans or shrieks, knowing
why the attendants wear rubber-soled shoes
and whisper.

Celeste sleeps, nested in bed in the middle
of traffic. Hour by hour easing her frame toward
the side of the bridge where she was left,
a flattened clump of feathers.
Reaching the edge with a crack like a shell
breaking open.
She huddles, shivering and blinking, hoping someone
will find her.

5.   Out of the Body

Celeste drifts   a luminous reflection
into the local railroad station   a black-
capped conductor sells tickets   she imagines
a country with no pear trees   or chickens
or children   frightened
she longs for any arms   even her own
cold ones   she wants to return
to skin and bone   chop her way
out of silence   howl at the dark

6.   Cherie Visits Her Friend in the Morgue

Celeste, the hair stylist at La Tresse,
spent eight hours a day on her feet.
Varicose veins grew swollen and thick,
branching entanglements of vines
in a jungle of flesh, always concealed
by slacks. Day by day the body
goes, almost imperceptibly,
tracings added like circles to a tree.
Look at her eyes for the date of her birth.
The face is a mask. It can be altered,
lifted, patched and plastered. Nothing
can change the cave of the eye, a dark
corridor death enters into

and when it exits through the open
mouth the head is thrown back,
the jaws are left gaping for the spirit
to follow. Cherie, so versed
in ungainly acts of love,
can appreciate the body's
grace in the rites of death.

Lang Anh's Daughter

1.   At Night

At night I am a passenger
in a ferryboat crossing the river.
I wear blue cotton pants
and a loose blue jacket.
My black hair is cut short.
I am going to visit my mother.
The boat appears to move forward,
the morning sky swallows its stars,
but time slips back,
unwinding as if from a spindle.
I am a child, my eyes
follow my mother as she
prepares our evening meal.
> The sun is sliding, the moon
> begins its flight. But the sun
> and moon are only my mother.
> Why should I ever leave her?

2.   Lang Anh Says Goodbye to Her Daughter

Fish rise:
sit on the barnacles of trees
or dive back into black
chunks of water.
You and I are those fish.
We have silver scales.
Our mouths bend down.
Our eyes are wide open.
Because there are two of us
we can swim underwater or fly.

No one can touch
the charged red thread that connects us,
the blood jet runs through.
Even when you're somewhere else
I wake to hear you breathe.

This is the valley of new bodies, old bones.
The defoliate trees are thin as skeletons.
I would like to keep you from learning
that the soil is dry ash and barren,
that love sowed in these fields
will not bloom
or crickets fold their long arms to pray.

Certain mutants have spread over the land.
Their heads are too large,
their bodies small
and brittle as shells
with nothing inside.

To take with you on your journey
I will give you a sharp tool of anger
to turn over the soil,
a few compassionate grains
to make the earth
darker and richer.
It's a beginning.
It's the best I can do.

At the Center for Displaced Persons

1.

With no common language, it's easy
to pretend we don't understand those
messages scrawled on thin leaves
of paper. They float in the distance
between us. Soon the *khamsin* will blow,

the dark desert wind. We feel it
in the air, try to avoid the shaft
of eyes, the attack of invisible ants.
The children are throwing flowers
that turn to a volley of stones.

In the hall a fistfight breaks out.
No one will die. We are all survival
experts, tramping out fuses before
a vital explosion. But the bitter
smell of smoke remains.

2.

We're waiting
for our vines and fig trees
to come by Railway Express.

The mails are slow.
We need toothpaste
            Italy
            cafés
            Chablis

                    Poland
                    stamps
                    scotch tape
                    France
We want to dance
wearing peasants skirts and velvet pants.

Are we asking too much?

3.

Overhead the sky
begins to wind like a windmill.
The slow grind of sand.
The coarse grains deform us.
We look
grotesque,
sideshow freaks
in the untimely
twilight.

Our images melt in the heat,
voodoo dolls bleeding
drops of wax. It's a curse
that makes us bend in the wind
adapt
        blend
                integrate
                        easily.
This is also our talent.

We mix with sand—
with each other
we are cryptic, aloof.

With no common language,
with the interpreter gone,
gathered in heaps rootless
as tumbleweed
we are lost,
too far from what we remember
to want to be close to anyone here.

The Victims

If I could I would
fall across steel

tracks to prevent the inevitable
from coming upon them. There is
no stopping mutilation, scattered
coats, mittens and legs spread

over black snow, the jackal packs
waiting in the shadows. Knowledge
gathers in the soles of my feet,
galaxies of electrons accelerate

like Strauss waltzes with infinite
energy. *Watch!* No way to explain
the fractured second when it is
possible to leap to one side, and so

useless, a show with no hero
or heroine. The untried crowd sighs,
disperses. No way to tell how I
could have avoided these amputations,

losses. No words for what
the body, alone, knows.

A Formal Feeling—

When they pulled the Persian rug
from under our father's feet, he fell

through a hole in the foundation.
Sixty candles on his layered cake
blew out. We children watched him go

as if he were playing the leading role
in our favorite Punch and Judy show.
We waited for the curtains to close,

slow red velvet. The doctor
came and wrote sixty certificates
that said he would never return

from the center of the earth.
The diggers arrived to lay
new floors, shiny boards, slippery

as a sliding pond. They slammed
the door as they departed, leaving
an arrangement of shriveled wreaths

and an invisible hole to guard.
Then we turned into stalks of ice
transfixed for sixty years, while

mice nibbled the candy in the cups
and dust covered our hair.

The Old Whore

Leech of my life, she glues
her thick torso to mine,
blows garlicky breath in
my ear, nags, "Walk faster.
We're late." She tells me I

won't ever get a job
or keep one, even with
four clocks next to the bed.
Hurrying down the street
she looks back, says

a bearded man wearing
a zebra skin and a gold
earring is following,
surely planning to rape/
kill me, whichever comes

first. Although anything
would be better than the
malignancy she knows
I'm programmed for. I'm apt
to talk fast, letting my

eyebrows hop around and
hoping no one will hear
her squealing at me or
notice her hectic blue
eyelids and tricolored

hair. I want to tell them,
"Listen, that isn't my
mother, clinging to my
shoulders like a moth-eaten
fox collar stolen from

Good Will." But by now I'm
used to the old bitch, my
life would be dull without
her, slung around me, her
teeth sunk deep in my neck.

Birthday

It is important to wait for the first croak
of our rooster. Greet the day! Greet
the day! Then I can sleep, but holding
an elephant in my hand. Mother is up,
scrambling eggs, a lady who never dreams.
How can she pretend to understand me. Oh
I catch the graffiti she tries to hide
under her lids. She thinks I don't notice.
Mother! There is no escaping what
we are when our mothers are with us.

We ride the subways, IRT, BMT, idling
on platforms, changing trains. We visit
the graves of dead cousins in Brooklyn.
She says, Are they happy? Do you think
they know what we're doing? We empty
our pockets, looking for tokens. Mine
contain chewing gum wrappers, shreds
of tobacco. Mother, why do we travel

together like this and always alone?
She has taken an escalator down to where
I can no longer see her. My passport
is not in order. They won't allow me
to follow. Easy for them to laugh
at me, a grown woman, crying for her
mother like a homesick child at camp.
I'm afraid without her I will lose
gloves, manuscripts, even the map of my
destination in the dim chambers underground.

Elegy for Mrs. Lucky

Who looked fragile and velvety
but who resisted insects and blight

and baked *pugachel* with nutshells
in them. Who wore a pince-nez
chained around her neck and spoke

of the novels of Anthony Trollope;
how with a top hat, empty sleeves,
and flights of insightful passion,

he told the truth about illusion.
How when you hold words by their
ears in front of a magic lantern

they disappear, or grow clearer,
as prisms twist and shimmer from
a crystal chandelier. How the deaf

use their hands to sign in haiku,
leaves fall, water moves, and on
the water, birds screech and creak

at our rude intrusion. When the hands
are gone, such brush strokes linger.

Facing It

The Inquisitor of the Past is Miss Burtsel,
a clean handkerchief pinned to her sleeve.
She has several voices, old familiars,

ticking and tocking accusations and threats.
She locks you in your room, alone.
Your cheeks are streaked with ancient tears.

Even the walls are bleeding. Outside
Mr. and Mrs. Robin gather twigs for their nest,
hippity-hoppity, twitter and frisk.

What you're looking for out here is a kind
word from the garbage man. You'd be his slave
forever, only he regards you as so much rubbish.

Sunbeam Bread wrappers, chicken bones, stacks
of *Good Housekeeping* and *Ladies Home.*
   YOUR GARBAGE OVERFLOWS THE CAN AGAIN.
He frowns, and you tremble with fear like

Sweet Alice, Ben Bolt. The sun falls down.
Thunder arrives, the sound of two cans clanging.
The truck groans darkly. You're left alone.

And the gift-wrapped hours you've waited for—
time to study chair caning or ornithology—
left like half-eaten tv dinners the neighbor's

dog finds among the ruins and finishes.
Your dirty trays litter the street.
The neighbors, despairing, shake their heads,

knowing you will never, never learn.

Falling into the Moment

Everyone is disappearing,
you must be getting older, you are

stripping, one by one, your leaves.
You begin to give away books,

bracelets, your comb collects hair,
freckles pepper your hands.

Your body repels you, the mirror
no longer casting a spell.

Yet, even now, when you let yourself
fall into one of the moments

you are trying to rush through,
you find yourself in a small boat

paddling channels, gathering lilies,
the sun settling on the water.

An experiment in light, a kind
of chemistry, a simple radiant equation.

Final Conjuring

You have learned everyone's
name and what the red and gold

lozenges of Harlequin
signify and the saffron

satins of Lady Wortley
Montagu. Entrances and

exits are smooth peppermint
extract you guzzle between

scenes. At last you have sixteen
Indian clubs whizzing in

air together. You turn to the
spectators. They are all

leaving. *Wait*, you call, holding
out your freckled hands. Sixteen

clubs drop to the boards. *Wait! Wait!*
The proscenium grows dim.

Your limp grin, suspended, spins
a chrysalis over the departing.

About the Series

Rites of Strangers is the third volume of poems to appear through the VCU Series for Contemporary Poetry, and was selected as the best collection among many hundreds judged by the distinguished poets serving as readers for the Associated Writing Programs. Fourteen poets residing in every region of the United States served as initial readers for collections which were submitted directly to them, and they recommended worthy books to a second reading committee whose task it was to reduce two hundred publishable manuscripts to two dozen. Each manuscript was read at least three times, and often as many as five different readers offered written opinions about every collection, finally narrowing the recommended books to twenty-four volumes, which were given to Elizabeth Bishop for final consideration. Rites of Strangers was Ms. Bishop's first choice, and was edited by Walton Beacham, General Editor for the VCU Series for Contemporary Poetry, in conjunction with the author. Each fall manuscripts are invited for consideration, and at least one volume is published through the VCU Series every year.

About the Author

Phyllis Janowitz is a native of New York. She is the winner of the 1977 Emily Dickinson Award, the 1977 Alfred Kreymborg Award, and the 1977 Bernice Ames Award. She is the author of two other books of poetry and her poems have appeared in such national publications as Atlantic Monthly, Esquire, and the Nation.